An Analysis
of an Important Text:

The World Health Organization's
Understanding of Health

Richard Grawath

Published by Richard Grawath

ISBN 978-1-4710-8319-8

An Analysis
of an Important Text:

The World Health Organization's
Understanding of Health

Author Information

RG has worked as a consultant, banker, analyst, researcher, author, teacher and university lecturer.

His qualifications provide the basis for his scientific and professional work:

Postgraduate Dip. in Medical Physics, M.Sc. in Science, M.B.A., Dip. in Psychology, B.Sc. (Honours) in Health Studies, B.Sc. (Honours) in Health & Social Care, University Cert. in Managing Care, University Cert. in Promoting Health, University Cert. in Reflective and Evidence-Based Practice, University Cert. in Health & Social Care.

Description

The World Health Organization provides a "definition" of health which is open to wide interpretations. It is a statement which may serve as a tool to justify economic and political actions. The statement claims to be valid for the whole world. These political actions may not consider the health of the populations as a priority but instead they seek increasing profits and power for a small group of ruling psychopaths as the main objective.

Table of Contents

Preface

This book is based on a talk which the author gave at the Philosophical Society in Malta on 3rd April 2019. The talk had the title "Can We Ever Be Healthy?"

The so-called "definition" of health of the WHO is in fact a statement. This has implications for the development and performance of health care systems on national levels and ultimately on a global level through the member countries in the WHO.

When can the WHO declare a pandemic? Since the WHO statement mentions absence of disease it is relevant to define what disease, physical and mental disease are. Who determines what a disease is? Can mental diseases be used to declare a population unfit to make economic and political decisions? Is it possible to construct a situation in which non-infectious diseases could be used to declare a pandemic? This would have enormous advantages for certain interest groups.

The Covid-19 crisis is mentioned only a few times in this book. Some critical investigations into the Covid-19 crisis concentrate specifically on the Covid-19 crisis subject and provide high quality assessments about it. The Corona-Ausschuss (The

Corona Investigative Committee) with Dr Reiner Füllmich and Viviane Fischer delivers exceptional insights into the crisis and the wider framework. Dr Wolfgang Wodarg is another founding member of the committee and there are numerous specialists from a panoply of professions who have contributed to the work of the committee.

Catherine Austin Fitts, James Corbett and others also conduct research and analyse the Covid-19 crisis.

Dr Vladimir Zelenko was a medical practitioner who developed his protocols for the prevention and treatment of Covid-19. Dr Zelenko also made his insights available to the public. The Zelenko Lab has stated that they would continue the work of Dr Zelenko after his death.

The New Earth Manifesto is an organisation which provides a broad insight into actions which can contribute to creating a better world for coming generations.

The analysis of the "definition" of health provided by the WHO and how it could be used to justify inhumane political and economic actions in the future is the main subject of this book. Some examples from the past aide the analysis.

In this book no medical advice is given and there are also no recommendations for a particular existing health care system.

April 2022

Richard Grawath

r.grawath@mailfence.com

Abbreviations

ADHD	Attention Deficit Hyperactivity Disorder
AI	Artificial Intelligence
AQI	Air Quality Index
ASR (World)	Age-standardised Rate (World)
BfA	Bundesanstalt für Arbeit (former German state agency for employment, and also for state pensions)
CI5	Cancer Incidence in 5 continents
DDR	Deutsche Demokratische Republik (East Germany, formerly German Democratic Republic)
DSM-5-TR	The Diagnostic and Statistical Manual of Mental Disorders, Fifth Edition
EPA	Environmental Protection Agency
EU	European Union
FRA	European Union Agency for Fundamental Rights

HDI	Human Development Index
HDR	Human Development Report
MoA	Mechanism of Action
NACC-UDS 2005-2010	National Alzheimer's Coordinating Center Uniform Data Set (US)
NGO	Non-governmental Organisation
NHS	National Health Service in the UK
$PM_{2.5}$	fine particles in the air
PPP	Public Private Partnership
TID	Target Identification
UNDP	United Nations Development Programme
WHO	World Health Organization

A Suitable Philosophical Approach

In an attempt to define health one should test the definition by giving examples and then check whether or not the proposed definition passes the test. Health is not just a theoretical construct without any connection to reality. An approach confined to theory will lose its validity in the context of the complexity of health. Health is a complex construct and has many levels and dimensions.

".. he (Carnap) suffered from one of the standard occupational diseases of philosophers; his exposition wanders off into abstract symbolic logic without ever considering a specific real example." [1].

In the areas of health and medicine it is crucial to provide examples in order to test which statement or observation might be true or close to the truth.

Traditional Chinese medicine is coherent in its understanding of the individual and the respective circumstances of life [2]. Integration of many aspects of life in the understanding of the disease processes of the individual is a key aspect of the philosophy of traditional Chinese medicine [2].

The statement about health from the WHO refers to the absence of disease and infirmity but there is no generally accepted definition of disease. The same is true for infirmity. In addition, the understanding of disease constantly changes. Developments such as the wellness movement and holistic approaches are picked up like a fashion by the WHO and are kept subordinate to the dominant institutionalised Rockefeller medicine.

To promote well-being requires more than just talking about it and producing documents with nice pictures as done by the WHO.

The WHO tries to force the concepts of Western medicine on developing countries. The concept of well-being is firmly embedded in the culture of Asian countries such as Vietnam.

Traditional medicine in Asia is much cheaper compared to modern high tech medicine from the developed countries. High tech medicine is connected to particular public health systems which also provide control over populations.

Following these developments like a fashion serves several functions. Disguising the underlying purpose serves the purpose of enabling the WHO to implement the ideologies of highly influential groups such as certain NGOs which give huge sums of money to the WHO. The Bill and Melinda Gates Foundation is an example of such a highly influential NGO providing huge funds to the WHO. In India a programme funded by the Bill and Melinda Gates Foundation was found guilty of disregarding regulations and rules regarding clinical trials as stipulated by the governments in the US [3]. Seven children died in a trial of the HPV vaccines in India [3]. No connection between the vaccinations and the deaths of the children was officially established but ethical shortcomings were detected. As a result, the Bill and Melinda Gates Foundation was barred from India's immunisation programme [3]. The exclusion of the Bill and Melinda Gates Foundation from immunisation programmes in India lasted a few years and then the foundation reappeared in an immunisation programme in India [3].

The fashion approach to disease also keeps academia, practitioners and the public busy with how to assess and deal with the changes. It creates the impression that institutionalised medicine has delivered new insights whereas in reality ideologies are being implemented.

The definition of mental disease has undergone many substantial changes by dropping certain diagnoses, such as for hysteria, and creating new diagnoses such as Attention Deficit Hyperactivity Disorder (ADHD) and bipolar disorder. The use of the diagnosis ADHD is disputed on various grounds, such as students being bored by certain subjects, being occupied by specific issues, not paying attention to lessons or being very active at the same time but not having a disorder. Teenagers in particular may not pay attention to lessons at school because they might be busy with issues about friendship and sexuality, which is normal for that age group.

Attempts to measure health on an arbitrary scale which is based on the mechanistic approach of medicine are destined to fail.

The WHO was and still is far away from understanding health as a complex concept which includes spiritual, religious, psychological, traditional, political, economic and social aspects.

Health disparities exist globally and many factors such as history, socio-economic conditions, structural influences of the distribution of power and resources and biological differences contribute to these disparities [4].

These disparities can be observed between countries as well as within countries [4]. Causality between pathways of health determinants and outcomes possess a high degree of complexity [4].

Strategies for interventions still need extensive investigations since the scientific understanding of these strategies addressing inequalities in health are far from being complete [4]. The "definition" of health of the WHO was written decades before the study by Edwards & Ruggiero [4] and the WHO statement about health uses the term "complete" in this context.

The WHO does not understand what health and health interventions addressing inequalities are. This raises the question whether the WHO really knows what they are talking about and doing or not doing in this respect.

Ethical issues in preparing for an influenza pandemic should be observed [5]. In general, ethical considerations are crucial in the provision of health care [5]. The handling of the SARS outbreak in Toronto showed the severe consequences of failing to explicitly state the ethical issues involved in such a situation [5]. The morale of hospital staff declines, vulnerable groups are stigmatised, public trust declines, misinformation occurs and confusion occurs with respect to responsibilities and roles [5]. During such a situation fairness plays a crucial role [5].

Practice in decision making in health care has shown that agreement about the principles for fair decision making is rare [6]. Procedural fairness is used instead of having guidance about principles of fairness [6]. This may explain the bad performance of health care systems in times of crisis such as during a pandemic. This might be a failure on a national level as well as on international level and in particular the WHO is not placing enough emphasis on distributing fairness principles in health care around the globe. Fairness in the allocation of resources is important because the different groups of a population have different needs and it is unfair if one group receives preferential treatments while other groups have urgent medical conditions which are not met because the measurements employed are not suitable. Transparency and accountability are crucial for fairness in health and social care. For example a patient might get expensive cosmetic surgery which might not have medical urgency while cancer patients have to wait for their treatments. Opportunity costs occur in cases were resources are used for less serious cases while medically serious cases are neglected [7].

The WHO statement about health not considering the differences around the globe and dividing the global population in particular groups is not ethical since it serves the goal of dividing the populations into groups such as elderly people, disabled people and other groups which can never achieve health according to the WHO statement about health.

Then there are groups which theoretically could achieve health.

There is the claim that "UNDP's Human Development Index (HDI) has captured human progress, combining information on people's health, education and income in just one number. " [8].

In an attempt to measure health the HDI uses life expectancy at birth [8].

This is one measurement for all humans combining many different aspects of human life, environmental data and economic data. Despite its composition of so many different subjects and areas of life it does not consider any differences in religious, philosophical, social, political and economical systems. The macroeconomic problems of inflation, unemployment and economic growth can be tackled by central banks and governments in different ways [9]. Price-level stability, employment at a high level and output at a high level with a rapid growth rate are the major macroeconomic goals [10]. These priorities have shifted since the Employment Act of 1946 in the USA [10]. A trade-off between these goals cannot be avoided [10]. Fiscal policy includes government expenditure such as purchasing arms and this influences the overall spending in an economy which affects the GDP level [10]. This type of government spending may have a significant negative effect on the health of many populations in the event of war even though the government spending has contributed to a higher level of GDP.

The HDI however assumes a positive effect on population health when higher GDP levels are reached. Even different countries within the countries of the European Union have different priorities in their respective economic situations. Stability, growth and employment do not have the same priorities in Germany, Italy, Greece, Spain and Ireland. In the EU we have the contradiction that although the countries of the Euro zone have the Euro as their legal tender these countries may pursue different economic policies. Germany has been known for a long time to have stability as a priority and this is often at the expense of higher unemployment. Italy has an emphasis on low unemployment, thereby possibly compromising price stability.

The HDI appears to be an instrument which enables some interest groups to manipulate and present data in a form which serves the interests of particular groups such as the WHO and certain NGOs.

This can be seen in UNDP's prediction that it would take 200 years to overcome the 'economic gender gap' on a global level [8]. This is a highly speculative prediction and it remains unknown where the demographic, economic and political data for such a long term prediction come from. Here serious questions about the UNDP prediction arise in terms of science.

The official numbers for unemployment are manipulated by governments.

In Germany in order to lower the figures for unemployment the government offered educational programmes for long term unemployed. Thus the participating individuals were taken out of the long term unemployment statistics in Germany. This has been the practice in Germany for a long time, in particular before elections.

The stress and the detrimental health effects may have continued or were even magnified when individuals were told that they had no choice about participating in educational programmes if they did not want to lose their state unemployment benefits.

The author accompanied a friend to the state agency for work in Frankfurt where he was told that he had to do a full-time course in marketing. He explained that he had studied marketing and therefore an introductory course in marketing would not make any sense. The adviser of the state agency for work told him that he would not receive unemployment benefits if he refused to participate in the marketing course.

Long periods of expected schooling are also a way to lower the unemployment figures in the young adult groups. Schooling is a competitive environment in Germany where access to places for certain subjects are restricted to students with good grades. This situation may be extremely detrimental to the health of school children, and it is certainly not a good indicator for improvements in health.

There is a high rate of student suicide in China because not getting top grades limits their chances of getting into a highly rated university. Even though in other countries the outcomes for the health of students might not be so extreme there are other outcomes such as drug taking, alcohol and nicotine abuse which are also damaging health. This indicates that the stress at university may also be high and detrimental to health. As a consequence if economic indicators show that many people may be able to afford higher education then this is not necessarily transformed into a health benefit. In fact, the opposite might be true.

The HDI includes schooling measured in mean years spent in the state schooling system as well as the expected mean of years spent at school [8]. This is a controversial approach since the schooling system is largely based on the Prussian school system which prioritised producing obedient graduates for the civil service and the military. After the 2nd World War the Allies abolished the Prussian state exactly because of the qualities which are held in high regard by the Prussian school system. The Prussian school system can therefore be seen as an outdated system, not suitable to serve as an indicator for human development. There are, of course, certain things which are taught at school which help to promote health, but these things can be and also are taught outside of school. Education inside the school system is preselected by technocrats; therefore there is a high possibility of it being used to promote a globalist agenda which is mixed into the rest of the subjects taught.

At first sight it might appear good that there is one measurement. The HDI is a composite measurement which contains so many components that an extremely vast number of factors is influencing the values of the HDI. However it may remain a very difficult task to find the factors which caused the upward or downward movement of a particular HDI value. A higher HDI value is seen as a better value as explained by the HDI average for women being 6% below the average HDI value for men [8], but higher values might be achieved through negative events as can be seen in examples given later.

The HDI also serves a political agenda in the area of environmental issues. Almost everyone would agree that the environment has to be protected but the inclusion of certain aspects of a political programme in the HDI destroys transparency and facilitates manipulation.

Throughout the history of the earth carbon dioxide levels in the atmosphere have changed as have the forest areas. At least part of the changes may therefore occur naturally. Even though correlation may exist, it does not mean causation. There is no scientific proof that those changes, natural changes as well as human made changes, have an equal effect on human health on a global scale. Human health is influenced by many factors but creating an artificial rigid mix of factors is an arbitrary endeavour which serves to promote a global agenda.

For the HDI, carbon dioxide is deliberately picked out to support the political agenda of the carbon footprint. Other even more disastrous man-made aspects, such as the increase of methane in the atmosphere, are not considered. Methane is a naturally occurring gas, as is carbon dioxide. Methane is a product of the digestive system and cattle produce vast amounts of methane. A substantial reduction of cattle farming as well as of industrialised beef production could easily result in a vast improvement for the environment. At the same time animal protection would increase. But this is not done for political reasons. Methane is not mentioned in the *Human Development Indices and Indicators, 2018 Statistical Update.*

The WHO "Definition" of Health

The so called "definition" of health by the World Health Organization is given in its constitution:

"Health is a state of complete physical, mental and social well-being and not merely the absence of disease or infirmity." [11].

The WHO assumes that every individual around the world has an absolute identical understanding of what disease is, but as explained below there are many different ways of understanding what disease is.

According to Carl Jung, an archetype is a symbol and an image [12]. Both of these aspects of archetypes are located in the unconsciousness of the collective [12]. An archetype has particular aspects which are in the mind of most people but the details differ from individual to individual [12]. The term 'health' is such an archetype and so are 'disease' and 'infirmity'.

The WHO attempts to provide a global definition for the archetype 'health' and refers to two other archetypes in its definition. All three terms are archetypes and each of them differs in numerous details from person to person so there is no globally agreed upon understanding for any of these terms.

The existence of humans without theory of mind can be observed in the case of the autism spectrum disorder.

If a person would provide a definition or statement about health which lacks an understanding of the wide range of details of the three archetypes health, disease and infirmity then that person might be placed on the very advanced side of the autism spectrum. The WHO has provided an ice-cold statement about health which lacks any insight into the details of the three archetypes health, disease and infirmity.

A general practitioner states uncritically, *"In my experience, most people with chronic conditions aspire to physical, mental, and social well-being. Most of them acknowledge that they may never again attain such a state of health. Acceptance of this fact is part of the process of moving on with their lives. However, they will never be healthy. ... The 1948 WHO definition of health is therefore as valid today as it was when it was published ."* [13].

The WHO statement about health excludes many

groups from ever being able to achieve health. This creates a dependency on health specialists, medical experts as well as pharmaceutical and medical devices companies.

This also creates huge demands for medical products since patients are told by medical professionals that they should trust the medical professionals and in order to achieve health they have to take the prescribed medicines. Power is exerted over patients who believe the narratives of the pharmaceutical and medical devices industries and their cronies.

Several NGOs, such as the WHO and the World Bank, collect data about health and disease, or conduct analysis or provide carefully selected information which all point towards a globalist approach towards health.

The WHO's approach is based upon Rockefeller medicine. In 1912 a monopoly was established for allopathic medicine in the USA [14]. According to Dr Glidden, allopathic medicine is perfect for the military, child bearing, dentistry and operations [14]. Other medical systems are branded as quackery [14]. Allopathic medicine uses a reductionist approach. Dr Glidden compares it to Newtonian physics; things which can be measured exist and what cannot be measured does not exist [14].

Conventional medical treatments do not cure the disease, rather they manage disease [14].

Managing disease with pharmaceuticals does not cure diseases such as high blood pressure, depression and cancer [14].

The side-effects of anti-depressants are responsible for the deaths of many patients through suicide [14].

Moreover, Dr Glidden points out that MD directed medical treatment is the major cause of bankruptcy, also citing that iatrogenic causes are the leading cause of death in the USA [14].

Allopathic medicine is based on outdated science which ignores the multilevel human existence [14].

According to Ronald Davis an extreme point of view exists that a large number of pharmaceuticals produce benefits despite the fact that neither the targets nor the mechanisms of action are known for these pharmaceuticals [15].

Davis states that another extreme point of view demands that at an early stage in drug development the target should be identified (TID) and the mechanism of action (MoA) should also be clarified

27

because this knowledge produces benefits in the real world [15].

Davis argues that a perspective which is located between the two in his opinion extreme views, would be best [15].

Davis states that the approach which uses TID has the major disadvantage that a profound understanding of the disease is crucial for the production of benefits [15]. Failing TID approaches can be due to the lack of scientific evidence for a molecular target which is relevant for the disease while at the same time it is promising therapeutic benefits [15]. A large number of complex diseases exist for which only a few promising TIDs exist [15]. Alzheimer's disease is one of these complex disease where a TID has been identified but the development of a treatment has failed so far [15] .

Considering the debate about TID, MoA and the failure of the conventional science to produce benefits in cases where scientists thought that they had identified TID and MoA, it appears that conventional science has either failed or was based on wrong assumptions, wrong data or was simply corrupt. Medical practitioners and conventional scientists may not consider that the data supplied for research may deliberately be wrong.

Furthermore it is the Rockefeller medicine which has labelled practitioners of traditional medicine quacks, but when it becomes obvious that School Medicine cannot produce the required scientific evidence then this is rarely mentioned or even covered up.

In Rockefeller medicine and the associated science it is not only problematic to identify TID and MoA, it is also problematic to arrive at the right diagnosis.

An investigation into the misdiagnosis of Alzheimer's disease found 88 misdiagnosed patients and 438 correctly diagnosed patients based on data from NACC-UDS from 2005-2010 in the US [16]. According to an initial analysis 18.18% of the misdiagnosed patients received potentially wrong pharmaceuticals [16]. A further analysis concluded that up to 67.10% of the misdiagnosed patients may have received wrong medications [16]. Some of the misdiagnosed patients may have had treatable conditions and did not receive the right treatment [16]. The misdiagnosed patients wrongly received a stigmatising label with no positive perspective since Alzheimer's disease is a neurodegenerative disease which has no cure and it is progressive. In this situation patients may be pushed into a process with no positive prognosis causing extensive harm to the patients, their friends, their families and society as a whole.

The findings of a very influential study about Alzheimer's disease may have been doctored [17]. The study took place in 2006 and since then further research built on these tempered findings [17]. According to *Science* magazine an investigation found more than 70 possible manipulations in images in 20 scientific papers by Sylvain Lesné, an associate professor (University of Minnesota) and neuroscientist [17]. The findings of studies by Lesné created long lasting interest in a particular assembly of proteins as a TID in the research about a cure for Alzheimer's disease [17].

A systematic review published in 2022 investigated the influential hypothesis of depression and considered the relevant strand of serotonin research [18]. The systematic review found no satisfactory evidence for a causal relationship of lower concentration or activity of serotonin and depression [18]. Evidence for an association could also not be established [18].

The examples for continuing problems in drug development, manipulation of scientific data and misdiagnosis of diseases show that governments and the WHO fail to provide appropriate health care on a large scale.

The big pharmaceutical companies run the world, and medical freedom does not exist [14].

The European Union Agency for Fundamental Rights refers to the EU Charter of Fundamental Rights, Article 35, health care [19]. The FRA talks about rights with respect to preventive health care and medical treatments but this is only under the restrictions of national laws and national practices [19].

The comments provided by The European Union Agency for Fundamental Rights do not, as FRA itself states, have the status of law [19]. This means that these comments may serve to aid debates of all kinds but individuals or groups may not have any real legal benefit from these explanations.

One may state that the EU Agency for Fundamental Rights pretends to provide aid for patients but in reality there are few or no tangible benefits for patients.

The production of glossy brochures and nice looking websites might be a waste of money and resources which could have produced some benefits for patients if these resources would have been used wisely. The same principle of wasting resources appears to apply to the WHO.

Health in Different Societies

What is mental and social well being in the context of a statement which claims to have global validity?

In Vietnam religions and philosophies exist in which the ancestors are part of everyday life and people can have the graves of their ancestors in the backyard. This would be completely unacceptable in Germany and other Western countries.

In India some religious groups cremate their dead and the ashes are handed over to the Ganges. The Zoroastrians have towers where the corpses are offered to vultures. This is perfectly in line with the local definition of mental and social well-being.

Orthodox Jews have burial procedures which have been passed down from generation to generation. The dead bodies are treated with respect and there are specific materials and clothing for the dead bodies. The body has to be laid to rest in an undamaged condition as much as possible. Cremation is a complete no no for Orthodox Jews. Any diversion from their tradition causes upset to the families and other Orthodox Jews.

There are similar procedures for Moslems.

In the US some companies offer the production of artificial diamonds from the remains of human corpses.

Globally there are vast differences about mental and social well-being. This contradicts the impression of a globally binding "definition".

In developed countries with state health care systems the sick person has the role of a patient. The medical practitioners have the specialist role signalled by wearing a special outfit. The phrase "gods in white" has been used extensively to describe the special status of medical practitioners. The role of the patient is a passive one. The doctor/patient relationship is characterised by trust which the patient has towards the medical practitioner. Only during the last few years has a critical attitude towards the medical professions increased. Demand for services in health care is a demand for health and not a demand for particular treatments.

In the context of the pharmaceutical and medical devices industries this means that the industries develop products such as pills or MRI machines which are then used in the provision of health care services but according to the statement of the WHO these cannot deliver the health desired by the patients since in its constitution the WHO requires *"complete physical, mental and social well-being"* for health [11]. The practitioner referred to above has the insight that most individuals with chronic disease are not able to achieve such a state of health [13].

The statement of the WHO fits into a business model in which the large corporations produce drugs and medical devices but the final product "health" can rarely be delivered, if at all. This business model functions like a money generating machine since according to the WHO statement about health, the demand for health is endless.

The gatekeepers in the system are the large pharmaceutical and medical devices corporations and the health professionals. The power of the medical practitioner is much smaller compared to the power of the large corporations but they are often the willing executioners. In this system the individuals seeking health are seen as passive consumers.

In health economics the cost of the provision of services is investigated and justified. In the USA MRI machines are quite expensive while in Japan there is a ceiling for the cost of MRI machines. As a result MRI procedures are more expensive in the USA than in Japan.

Traditional medicine is much less expensive compared to modern high tech medicine. Side-effects of the modern chemical compounds can be quite dangerous and these side-effects regularly require other drugs to treat the side-effects of the first drug.

Aspirin has long been used and it was initially produced from the bark of a particular tree. Now Aspirin is produced on an industrial scale. The initial patent for Aspirin has expired but when a particular compound such as a vitamin is added then this new creation might be patented even though there might be no medical indication for such a combination. A new combination which includes an old drug as the active ingredient can then be sold at a higher price compared to the original drug for which the patent has expired.

Aspirin has long been used as a painkiller and one might think that it is harmless. It has also been used in low doses as a prophylaxis against stroke however more recent research has shown that bleeding in the stomach might occur quite often. Surprisingly, often the precise mechanism of active ingredients in pharmaceuticals is not known.

What is Disease?

Health as "*absence of disease*" means nothing because there is now another term in the WHO statement which needs a definition [11]. The question arises, "What is disease?". The nature, understanding and definition of disease has changed over time and it is still changing and subject to the manipulation of the powerful group of psychopaths which at the moment rules the world.

Social and psychological factors in mental illness may show variations across different countries [20]. Anorexia nervosa has a higher prevalence in developed countries compared to developing countries [20]. In Asia the presence of physical symptoms in depression is more common than in Europe [20]. This is an example of how cultures affect the ways symptoms are presented [20].

Some argue that addiction is a disease. Others point out that, at least at the beginning, there is the element of choice.

Hysteria is a controversial subject and feminists do not like the term. At the beginning of the 20th century the diagnosis of hysteria had the approval of the official science of the day and patients did not question the specialists who thought or pretended that they were impartial scientists. Similar things happen today.

The criteria for mental disease in the *DSM* are not intended to be used by the general public [21]. They are to be used by trained professionals [21]. This means the trained professionals claim ownership of the decision as to what a mental disease or disorder is and who is having a mental disease or mental disorder and who is not. The affected public is excluded from the pseudo-scientific discourse of the *DSM*. This is in contrast to some patient movements which state that the patients have a unique understanding of their disorder or disease. In the understanding of some patient movements the patient is the true specialist in this respect and the so-called disease might be an enrichment of their existence as a human. Thus labels should not be attached to them.

Unspecified Attention Deficit Hyperactivity Disorder (ADHD) 314.01 provides a category for which the psychiatric practitioner does not specify why the criteria for ADHD are not fully met [22]. This is dangerous because the psychiatric practitioner is enabled to attach a label to a person even though in those cases the symptoms may not exist but the psychiatric practitioner has the power to put a person into the specific pigeon hole ADHD. Labelling a person may have far reaching consequences and a lifelong history of mental treatments may follow a labelling based on a vague observation or even an exaggerated statement which otherwise would have been a meaningless short term behaviour or mood.

Another example for problematic issues in the *DSM 5* is the Specific Learning Disorder where the *DSM* states that only one of the diagnostic criteria is sufficient for the diagnosis, if the diagnostic criteria persist after 6 months of intervention [23]. The *DSM 5* (2013) lists 6 diagnostic criteria. Number 6 reads as follows: *"Difficulties with mathematical reasoning (e.g., has severe difficulty applying mathematical concepts, facts, or procedures to solve quantitative problems)*" [23]. The other 5 diagnostic criteria are also problematic [23] . If the psychiatric practitioner is particular petty then it is easy to attach a label which might stigmatise the individual even though that criterion is not causing any major problem for the individual. It is at least questionable whether a single criterion is really sufficient to attach a label to an individual who is otherwise not having any learning problems. Biological markers for the Specific Learning Disorder are not known [23]. Furthermore, the diagnosis cannot be based on findings obtained through neuroimaging, genetic testing or cognitive testing [23].

There is the danger that the *DSM 5* may provide a carte blanche to attach psychiatric diagnoses to a large number of individuals in a given population and use this as justification for economic and political purposes against groups or even populations.

This situation could be called psychiatric tyranny.

Demanding Complete Well-being

The use of the term "*complete*" in the WHO statement about health is located in the areas of being perfect and absolute [11]. The statement of the WHO has the intention of putting health out of the reach of the individual. It is a matter of definition what "*complete*" means. There are so many different individuals, groups, populations and areas around the globe so it is extremely hard or even impossible to provide a conclusive definition of "*complete*" within this context of human diversity.

If health cannot be reached by so many people then this can seen as promoting medication to people who are not in need of treatment because they are not sick [7]. The far reaching implications include putting labels on people, opportunity costs, waste of economic resources and treatment decisions which are poor or even wrong [7]. The occurrence of iatrogenic diseases may increase in such a situation [7]. Sickness which is being sold may create a situation in which people are obsessed with health to an unhealthy extent [7]. Using sickness in this way creates markets for all types of health and wellness products [7].

The business people behind the psychopathic use of sickness are ignoring the fact that health markets are different from all other markets in the sense that health is at the core of humanity.

The development of new drugs which are aimed, in principle, to treat healthy people is diverting funds away from dealing with real disease. This is critically damaging publicly funded health care systems where people are forced to pay into these health care systems which are used by business people who lack the most basic ethical and moral qualities of a normal individual [7].

Infirmity in the "Definition" of Health

The WHO refers to the absence of "disease or infirmity" [11]. Searching for the term "*infirmity*" in the *DSM 5* yields no result [11]. "*Infirmity*" has no precise scientific definition and the determination of who is infirm remains a matter of interpretation [11]. The online dictionary vocabulary.com explains that "*infirmity*" is a "*disability or weakness, especially due to old age*" [24].

An online medical dictionary states rather vaguely: "*being infirm, often associated with old age; weakness or frailty*" [25].

The reader of the WHO statement about health may subconsciously get the message that old age is not compatible with health. The WHO statement about health may therefore implicitly contain the statement that health cannot be achieved at old age. This may have consequences for rationing. Triage is a term which originates from the military but the practice of triage is now also used in non-military health care. In triage resources are first used for cases where the expected positive outcome is more likely compared to cases where a positive outcome has a high degree of uncertainty or might be impossible in the long run. The last aspect would mean that old people would not have a good chance of obtaining treatment if life expectancy is considered.

Religious Aspects

Health can only be achieved if both body and mind are in a balanced and good working condition. The idea of having a day of rest is now very common. Many states have laws about the number of working hours per week and days of rest. Even so, there might be no reference made to the Sabbath as the time of rest having been moved to Sunday in most countries.

The requirement of having running water for ritual baths is also connected to health.

Several regulations about food exist, including kosher food, which types of food must be kept separately or may not be eaten at all.

Very much connected to health is the concept of Pikuach Nefesh through which the health and life of a person should be preserved. This concept overrides all other regulations of the *Torah* and firmly places human life and health at the centre of Judaism. The following text in the *Torah*, Leviticus 18:5., can be seen as an implicit rule that saving life is paramount, *"You shall observe my statutes and my ordinances, which a man shall do and live by them. I am the Lord."* [26].

and also in the *Torah* Ezekiel 20:11 supports this idea: *"And I gave them My statutes, and My ordinances I made known to them, which, if a man perform, he shall live through them."* [27].

There are discussions in the *Talmud* about situations where the Pikuach Nefesh applies. The discussion continues about situations in which Pikuach Nefesh is justified.

This means that already in ancient times there was a holistic view of health.

The *New Testament* is the base for the large Christian religion and there are huge variations in the interpretation of its texts of the *New Testament*. Numerous different spellings and wordings of the texts exist.

The Greek text of the *New Testament* uses the term *"iatros"* which may be translated as physician. In a modern understanding of this term a formal recognition is implied so one may argue that healer might be a better translation. Even a few thousand years ago some formal recognition might have existed, even though the criteria might have been different. Evidence of healing was most likely a key issue and from a modern point of view this type of evidence was a subjective criterion.

The healing narratives in the *New Testament* can be seen as attempts to prove that Jesus might be the Messiah. This is a matter of belief.

Mark 2.17 reads as follows: *"When Jesus heard [it], he saith unto them. They that are whole have no need of the physician, but they that are sick: I came not to call the righteous, but sinners to repentance."* [28].

The Wider Frame of Health

Health is the subject of medicine, psychology, psychiatry and the sciences; not only the natural sciences, but also history, economics, politics and most crucially philosophy. The understanding of health is based on an individual's and the society's understanding of human existence, its view of the world and its underlying values.

Corporate governance has implications for the economy and the social well-being [29].

Rationing is common practice in modern medical health care systems and it could be argued that it is immoral. Some companies make huge profits while some people are excluded from the provision of medical health care. Numerous alternative therapies, such as the Gerson Therapy, are not approved in the US and other countries and therefore they are not available in those countries.

It could be argued that the demand for health care is in fact a demand for health. This is a particular view in which the human is a consumer who is 'buying' health. The responsibility for health is ultimately moved to the group level since providers of medical health care need formal approval. This means that decisions about health and what it is have become the domain of the group rather than the domain of the individual. Self-determination with respect to health is fought by the dominating Rockefeller medicine model.

Randomised controlled trials are the gold standard for the use of a pharmaceutical in medicine. This suggests a scientific way for restoring health.

Regulations have been put in place which state which treatments are recognised and are therefore allowed to be provided whereas other treatments are excluded. Here the understanding of what science can prove or not prove and how the processes of approvals can be influenced are crucial. The limitations of science in the context of health are obvious but these limitations are covered by phrases such as 'it is assumed'. Scientists create hypotheses which build upon theories.

What if it turns out that the diastolic blood pressure value is more important in the diagnosis of high blood pressure?

In the past it was assumed that neurons could not be

replaced but it has turned out that they can indeed be replaced.

The consequence is that human ideas about natural categories do not provide a definition of what the thing really is.

So the question arises: "Is health a concept?" For categories there are measurements for the central tendency of a population called a prototype. What is the prototype of health, or a "completely" healthy human in the context of the WHO statement about health?

Some people are heavy smokers and live, at least by widely accepted standards, 'unhealthy' lives but die at biblical ages e.g., Helmut Schmidt, a former chancellor of Germany, and his wife. Both were heavy smokers and Helmut Schmidt also used to snuff tobacco.

Other people do not smoke, do not drink alcohol, eat healthy food and die at a young age of cancer or some other disease.

There are too many borderline cases in the concept approach of health.

The prototype theory has the problem that the context plays an important role in typicality effects.

Here are just some examples:

Sickle cell anaemia is a disease which has a higher prevalence in particular countries with large exposure of the populations to malaria. Lighter skin colour is more prevalent in Northern Europe. Certain cancers have different prevalence, incidence and mortality in different geographical areas.

Mental Disease and Institutions

Lennox Castle Hospital was the largest mental institution in Scotland [30]. The Hospital opened in 1936 and closed in 2002 [30]. The patients there were categorised as mentally deficient [30]. There were patients who had no mental disorder, such a confused teenagers, and abuse occurred there on a regular basis [30]. When institutions such as Lennox Castle Hospital were closed the health services did not go through a learning process [30].

In Lennox Castle Hospital the patients were kept like inmates in a prison. Similar constructs exist in modern mental health care.

In Lenox Castle Hospital the number of patients reached a peak of 1,500 and patients from 10 years of age to 80 years old were housed in the hospital [31]. Several hundred corpses of adults and several dozens of children who were patients in mental hospitals were buried in mass graves up to 1975 [31]. These burials were done by the state and now after so many years there is little or no possibility to determine the circumstances of their medical treatments or histories, deaths and burials. Did these patients or their relatives give consent to all of this? Other cases of common burials of corpses from children in mental institutions exist [31]. Hundreds of unmarked graves of children from orphanages are also known to exist in Scotland [31]. This was common practice in the NHS, the state health service in the UK [31]. In addition, institutions run by nuns who were accused of abuse and beating their patients had the same practice of burials for their patients [31]. Evidence suggests that medical experiments were performed on disabled children in state care [31]. These are historical examples from the NHS practice. Could it be that medical practice is performed according to what the culprits can get away with at any particular time? How many cases of medical malpractice are unknown and are performed at present?

It has been claimed that pharmaceutical trials and psychiatric experimentation in Scotland were linked to the CIA [31].

Meaningless phrases such as 'congenital idiocy' and 'organic brain disease' were given as causes of death for children [31].

Nowadays fancy sounding phrases are used and new creations are presented as scientific facts.

In addition to the above examples there was also the race theory which was used during the 3rd Reich to justify scientifically the application of euthanasia.

According to Salize, Dreßing and Peitz, when coercive measures in psychiatry are applied then a balance between public safety, the particular person's human rights and the need for appropriate treatment have to be balanced [32]. Some authors observed a correlation between compulsory admission rates and available beds in psychiatric institutions [32], [33], [34]. In 1996 the WHO stated that mental health law should follow 10 principles [32]. Critics pointed out that these guidelines counteract the rights of patients and justify medical power using coercion [32], [35], [36], [37]. A lack of proper information given to patients who were compulsorily admitted and patients not knowing that appeal procedures exist has been observed [32].

The diagnoses of depression, mania, schizophrenia and various different psychotic disorders are found much more often in people who are compulsorily admitted to psychiatric institutions [32]. In the group of compulsorily admitted organic psychosis, substance abuse or personality disorders are much rarer [32]. In the context of the diagnoses referred to above several studies confirm this finding [32], [38], [39],[40].

In Germany Beate Bahner, a lawyer, criticised the Covid-19 measures of the government and in 2020 she was compulsorily admitted to psychiatric examination [41]. Ms Bahner has worked as a lawyer for about 25 years and she is a specialist lawyer for medical law [41]. The police handcuffed Ms Bahner and forced her to the ground. So far there has been no disagreement about this incident in the reports by Ms Bahner and the police [41]. The police brought her to a psychiatric institution in Heidelberg where a medical doctor decided that Ms Bahner had to stay [41]. The psychological sickness aide law (Psychisch-Kranken-Hilfe-Gesetz (PsychKHG)) of the German state of Baden-Württemberg provided the basis for the following official actions undertaken from that point onwards [41]. Was this case a test for future situations where people who criticise the government simply end up in a psychiatric institution?

Ms Bahner was forcefully admitted without a ruling from a judge and this activity may have had the purpose of silencing a critical voice [42]. Ms Bahner complained about police brutality, denial of access to a lawyer and restrictions of freedom [42].

According to Goldhagen, the police were complicit in the holocaust as well as other atrocities [43]. Goldhagen lists many police battalions and regiments in the index of his book *Hitler's Willing Executioners* and these entries often refer to negative events such as major killings, shootings and deportations of victims to various death camps [44].

During the 3rd Reich physicians were complicit in mass murder and other atrocities [45]. In this context Goldhagen refers to the book *The Nazi Doctors: Medical Killing and the Psychology of Genocide* by Robert Jay Lifton (New York: Basic Books 1986) [45]. Goldhagen (1996) also refers to the book *Euthanasia in the National Socialist State: The Destruction of Unworthy Life (Euthanasie" im NS-Staat: Die "Vernichtung lebensunwerten Lebens)* by Ernst Klee, Fischer Verlag, Frankfurt, 1983 [45]. The German expression "lebensunwerten Lebens" literally means "worthless life", a phrase which is used nowadays in some variations such as "useless eaters" and "unworthy life".

In general all professions were corrupted in the 3rd Reich [45]. Many countries have gone through this before, meaning it is not a new phenomenon.

In a medical tyranny who is going to decide who is allowed to live? Medical martial law is inhumane by its nature because there is a lack of basic human rights, a lack of transparency, a lack of justice and no right to appeal.

The critical reader will be able to discover parallels between the situation in the 3rd Reich and the current crisis.

Anonymous Health Administration

Nowadays the individual is confronted with an inhuman public administration system. The staff administering the rules do not want to take responsibility for their actions. In addition there is no real accountability despite the fact that the public has to pay for the public administration system. Transparency is also non-existent.

In corporate governance the agency theory puts the shareholder in a special position whereby shareholders are the residual risk carriers while the question of ownership may not be relevant [29]. Small shareholders as such are investors who bear the residual risk without a guarantee of benefit from their investment. This puts them in a situation where they have to take losses but are unfairly treated in terms of benefits such as dividends and participation in decision making with respect to the firm in which they invested. This may be a frustrating and unhealthy situation in times of economic problems. In addition small shareholders have to pay contributions to the social systems of the state with limits on how to reduce these expenses. In particular in Germany the employed small shareholder has to pay contributions to health insurance, long term care, unemployment insurance and state pension insurance. In addition taxes are high in Germany. VAT is 19% and other taxes consume substantial percentages of the income of small shareholders and other employed staff so that there is little left for out of pocket payments for treatments which are not approved. The system is set up so that real choices are severely limited and this is a very unhealthy environment in terms of freedom and well-being.

Clarke (2004) refers to Simon Learmount (2002) when he analyses the Anglo-American understanding of the firm in terms of economic theory [29], [46]. The economic theory in the Anglo-American understanding of the firm has three basic assumptions [29]. First the firm is understood in contractual terms, second human behaviour is directed by utility maximisation and self interest, and third the protection of invested capital is a 'corporate governance problem' [29] .

The Anglo-American concept of the firm can be applied to the health care system in the form of Public Private Partnerships (PPP). As a consequence contradictions in a PPP coexist between a state welfare system and private sector firms and are more likely to be resolved in favour of the Anglo-American understanding of the firm because of the dominance of contractual terms. This would mean that constellations in the PPP do not have the population's health at the centre of their activities. The firms participating in a PPP have huge benefits, such as guaranteed number of 'customers', laws and contracts tailored to the needs and wishes of the firm and access to data. In the case of a PPP the people are not really 'customers' since they cannot opt out of compulsory state health insurance, for example in the NHS in the UK. In Germany only people above a certain income have the option to switch from the state health insurance to a private health insurance. This may be cheaper at a young age but might have disadvantages if the person becomes unemployed and has to stay in the private health insurance which might not be paid for by the unemployment benefits. The state health insurance systems tend to pay only for approved treatments and may also pay a certain percentage of particular treatments. The private firms in PPP have their contracts made to measure and are able to put pressure on the public sector part of the PPP. If the private firms have specific wishes for changes in the contracts then the public part of the PPP seems to be more than willing to accommodate the wishes of the private firms. In case of disputes the public administration may be completely unable to take over the parts of the health systems managed by firms due to artificially created barriers such as contractual obligations, complex networks of participating firms and cronyism. This mix of the private and public sectors is reducing transparency and making it difficult to allocate responsibility. In this way the firms can hire consulting firms and may be able to burden the public sector with additional expenses. Anonymity is created which may benefit the public administration and the firms. Public health systems may be systematically starved of funding so that an artificially created emergency can be created which in turn may be used to justify the introduction and existence of a PPP.

Rationing has been used for decades in the public sector health systems and it has been justified by artificial emergencies, expensive bureaucratic procedures and underfunding. The different parts of the PPP act in a type of concerted action whereby no part accepts responsibility for mismanagement and mistakes.

Marcuse described this situation:

"The real ghost is of a very forcible reality - that of the separate and independent power of the whole over the individuals. And this whole is not merely a perceived Gestalt (as in psychology), nor a metaphysical absolute (as in Hegel), nor a totalitarian state (as in poor political science)- it is the established state of affairs which determines the life of the individuals." [47].

Currently we have a mixture between 'the established state of affairs' as described above by Marcuse [47] and a totalitarian system in which democracy has been eliminated. The abolishment of democracy is disguised so that most citizens are not aware of the lack of democracy such as in the cases of rigged elections.

Here I want to give examples from my own experience. I lived in Malta for about 5 years. During that time I had private health insurance. I went to the Mater Dei Hospital which is the only large state hospital in Malta and I inquired about the documents which I would need if I were to require emergency treatment at that hospital. I was informed that I would need the plastic card from the health insurance company and a letter from the insurance company stating that they cover emergency treatment. About 2 months later I got something in my eye and I could not remove it, so I went to that hospital for emergency treatment. A friend of mine accompanied me and at the reception desk of the hospital I was told that the rules had changed and that in addition to the plastic card from the health insurance company I now needed the last 6 payment slips from my employer. The woman at reception insisted on her demands and she refused to give her name. Her name badge was lying upside down on the desk behind the security glass cage. When I insisted that she provide me with her name she called security and I was told that I could file a complaint at the customer care desk. My friend and I went to the customer care desk but they refused to accept my complaint there. I was forced to return home and the next day I went to a private health clinic and had the particle removed.

The lack of transparency, accountability and responsibility is not confined to health care. It is endemic to all public services in the so-called "highly developed countries".

At the time of the DDR I travelled to Berlin and I spoke to a member of staff of the BfA there. At that time this was the organisation for the administration of the state pensions. Now the "Arbeitsamt" is called the "Agentur fuer Arbeit" and the people who have to pay into the state pension system are now called "customers". Back then, before the rebranding of that organisation, I had a lively discussion with a member of staff of the BfA who was a civil servant. I explained to him that the state pension system uses too much money for the administration of the funds. The majority of the population would be much better off without the BfA and that I would like to try to get my payments out of the system which I had been forced to pay into the system. I intended to live outside Germany and later, at retirement age, I would have more money available if I could manage my own pension funds. I said if required I would sue the staff whose names were given on the print-outs of the BfA. He replied that these names are not real names. They are pseudonyms and if someone tries to sue the staff of the BfA, the BfA would simply state that staff with those names are unknown to the BfA. Thus a private person would have no legal claim at all. He also said that a private person would have no real reason to file a claim since the BfA does not make any mistakes. Such hubris seems to be widespread within the public administration in Germany.

Here is another quote from Marcuse in which he captures the situation described above:

"However, the way in which such things and people are organized, integrated, and administered operates as an entity different from its component parts-to such an extent that it can dispose of life and death, as in the case of the nation and the constitution. The persons who execute the verdicts, if they are identifiable at all, do so not as these individuals but as "representatives" of the Nation, the Corporation, the University." [47].

In this context one may observe what I call the silent aggression of the technocrats. This silent aggression may also be observed in the inappropriate smiles of billionaires and their cronies in situations such as funerals or discussions about genocide, war and war crimes.

The state health care systems follow their own laws and procedures which suit their interests and also suit the interests of large corporations and NGOs, but do not serve the health care needs of the populations. The executioners of the laws and rules may enjoy the power which they obtain through the particular level at which they are allowed to practice. In the technocratic era they make decisions in a digital prefabricated manner, thereby paving the way for AI. This is inevitably leading to a complete exclusion of human considerations and at the advanced stage of technocracy the executioners will inevitably become redundant. The executioners will end up as victims of their own success if they are not stopped before AI rules over humanity. Alienation of the population can be observed since the executioners are also the ones who make the rules and laws which do not reflect the needs of the populations.

The concept of implicit consent was introduced in the NHS in the UK. This means if the patient does not explicitly express a particular idea, wish or concept then the NHS staff may assume that the patient has consented to the treatments as planned by the NHS staff. Marcuse also sees the wider frame of this NHS assumption which reduces the human mind:

"If I speak of the mind of a person, I do not merely refer to his mental processes as they are revealed in his expression, speech, behavior, etc., nor merely of his dispositions or faculties as experienced or inferred from experience. I also mean that which he does not express, for which he shows no disposition, but which is present nevertheless, and which determines, to a considerable extent, his behavior, his understanding, the formation and range of his concepts." [47].

This means that the mind of an individual not only contains what this individual explicitly expresses but also what he does not explicitly expresses. There is also a selection process of concepts based upon individual human experiences, intuitions, emotions, learned abstract facts and human preferences. This creates a far more complex existence and makes it far more difficult to understand this complexity. AI may have a hard time or may even be unable to understand the complexity of the human mind.

Modern societies concentrate on the physical aspect of human existence which can be measured and evaluated while neglecting all other aspects of human existence. *"The two layers or aspects of objectivity (physical and historical) are interrelated in such a way that they cannot be insulated from each other; the historical aspect can never be eliminated so radically that only the "absolute" physical layer remains."* [47].

This expresses the importance of tradition for human societies. Tradition includes knowledge of the past, wisdom, religion, philosophy and the different ways in which humans live all over the globe. There are positive and negative aspects, but this has produced a richness of existence and developments of societies which have never stopped. There is no single human or small group of humans which knows what is best for all humans, either here and now or in the future. The WHO statement about health ignores the historical aspects of health, including traditions of healing, different developing social structures and understandings of health and disease.

There are different ecosystems and different climate zones. Food sources differ from place to place as well as does the water, the elevation of the land and the distribution of the chemical elements.

Food is different in different areas and it often forms part of a country's national identity as it is closely connected to a country's health, traditions and economy.

What is the Purpose of the WHO?

The quality of the air humans breathe should be one of the top priorities of the WHO.

The air quality in Beijing has been measured by the US Embassy there using the Air Quality Index (AQI) with a scale used by the Environmental Protection Agency (EPA) in which 500 is the intended maximum value on this scale. Nevertheless the value for Beijing was 755 [48].

The WHO has been in existence for several decades but it has obviously failed to prevent this enormous health hazard for one of the largest populations on Earth. One has to ask why the WHO did not officially reprimand the Chinese government for this health hazard affecting such a large population. The US embassy obtained and published this extremely high value for the AQI for Beijing. The WHO sounded an early alarm for Covid-19 based on a very small number of cases but in the case of the AQI measurement for Beijing the WHO failed to sound an appropriate alarm. One may assume that political considerations prevented the WHO from taking action. One may also assume that the WHO might not have the health of populations at the centre of its activities. There are also other sources of information about the high levels of pollutants in the air. In a study Guo et al found an increased risk for lung cancer incidence associated with an increase of fine particles ($PM_{2.5}$) in the air [49]. This shows that there is scientific evidence for demanding preventive action to be taken to reduce $PM_{2.5}$ in the air [49].

One may argue that the WHO cannot reprimand such a powerful country like China but the WHO has also failed to reprimand small countries such as the tiny state of Malta.

In 2020 in Malta, the Age-standardised Rate (World) [ASR (World)] for lung cancer incidence for men was 34.1 per 100,000, this being the second highest ASR (World) incidence rate of all cancers for men in Malta [50]. In Malta, the ASR (World) for lung cancer mortality for women was 16.7 per 100,000, this being highest ASR (World) mortality rate of all cancers for women in Malta in 2020 [50]. Considering the small size of the country, the 194 deaths from lung cancer for both sexes in Malta in 2020 place a high burden burden on the health care system and on the society in general [50]. In the same year, death from lung cancer for both sexes had the first rank [50]. In 2020 deaths from lung cancer was more than one fifth or 20% of all deaths from cancer for both sexes in Malta [50]. The government's approaches to lung cancer and Covid-19 appear to lack consistency since lung cancer has been a problem for many years in Malta yet it has not received nearly as much government intervention as did Covid-19.

Looking at the role of the WHO in the case of water quality, which is also essential for human health, one gets an equally bad picture for the WHO. This indicates that the WHO is looking only at some health outcomes. A more extensive investigation into the WHO in terms of health outcomes would probably yield an even darker picture.

According to the UN access to clean water is considered to be a human right but it seems to be that this human right is not really taken seriously by governments and the WHO [51].

In their 2018 report the WHO added 2 new health indicators:

- Mortality from unsafe water, unsafe sanitation and lack of hygiene [SDG 3.9.2]

- Mortality from unintentional poisoning [SDG 3.9.3]

Under the environmental risk factors they state:

- Population using safely managed drinking-water services [SDG 6.1.1] [52].

Malta is a Moloch in terms of air and water pollution. Malta's tap water is the second worst in Europe [53]. Several scientific studies about water quality show that the water quality in Malta is extremely low [53]. The WHO, however, has remained largely silent about this situation despite the apparent danger to the health of the Maltese population and the tourists visiting the tiny state in the Mediterranean Sea.

People in Malta are unduly exposed to health risks due to the bad quality of the tap water yet the Maltese government pretended to be concerned about public health during the Covid-19 crisis and quickly imposed strict measures. The extremely low tap water quality affects everyone who uses it and this particular risk has a high degree of certainty while the risk for a serious outcome of the Covid-19 infection probably has a much lower degree of certainty.

In Malta the quality of air is also of exceedingly low quality due to airborne pollutants [54]. In Malta the figure for death from air pollution is twice the values previously assumed [54]. According to a study published in the *European Heart Journal*, in the EU air pollution is responsible for about 800,000 premature deaths annually, with about 2 years of life lost for the average person [54]. Air and water pollution on this scale does not occur suddenly over night. Measures could have been implemented to prevent these extreme levels of pollution in the EU but neither the governments concerned nor the WHO prevented these bad situations. As pointed out by Thomas Münzel, while smoking can be avoided it is not possible for the individual to avoid exposure to air pollution [54].

Lung cancer has the first rank among preventable deaths [55]. In 2018 death from lung cancer in Malta continued to have the highest frequency of all deaths from cancer [55]. In 2020, with 16%, lung cancer in Malta had second place in the list of cancer sites for men [55]. A National Cancer Plan was launched for the second time in Mata [55]. Official statements provide interpretations suggesting progress however if real improvements can be observed then there might be a lack of a scientific proof for causality between a particular programme and the cancer data. A critical analysis of the available data may indicate an alibi function of the National Cancer Plans as mentioned later in this chapter. In 2019, approximately 4% of all deaths in Malta were attributed to exposure to ozone and $PM_{2.5}$ [55].

Globally, 91% of the human population was exposed to polluted air in 2016 [56]. For the same year it has been estimated that indoor and outdoor pollution of the air is responsible for about 7 million deaths worldwide [56].

When one analyses the lung cancer data and the devastating effect of lung cancer on a global level, the all encompassing approach of dealing with Covid-19 appears to be a totalitarian overreaction. When it comes to lung cancer, the governments of small countries such as Malta, the governments of large countries such as China as well as the WHO fail miserably.

In 2018, from all cancers worldwide, lung cancer had a 11.6% for incidence for both sexes [57]. For the same year lung cancer, the leading cause of cancer deaths, was 18.4% for men and women [57].

Furthermore, polluted air has a huge negative effect on human health and one cannot see substantial attempts in Malta or on a global level to reduce air pollution. Once again one is led to ponder the question why governments employ draconian measures when it comes to Covid-19 but are rather relaxed when it comes to large scale air pollution caused by corporations. These developments are not only disempowering for lung cancer patients but also for the majority of humans on Earth.

The importance of clean water and clean air have been known for thousands of years, but the WHO presents these well-established facts as if they have just found out about them. They act as if they are saving the world by making statements with no real actions taken to prevent bad situations.

Aristotle recognised the importance of clean water and air and in his book *Politics* he explains, *"And since we have to consider the health of the inhabitants, and this depends upon the place being*

well situated both on healthy ground and with a
healthy aspect, and secondly upon using wholesome
water-supplies, the following matter also must be
attended to as of primary importance. Those things
which we use for the body in the largest quantity,
and most frequently, contribute most to health ; and
the influence of the water-supply and of the air is of
this nature. Hence in wise cities if all the sources of
water are not equally pure and there is not an
abundance of suitable springs, the water-supplies
for drinking must be kept separate from those for
other requirements. " [58].

Aristotle was born in 384 BC and many of his
insights have fundamental value for all humans [58].
This means that his insights were documented over
2,000 years ago [58]. Since then numerous scientists
have conducted research into clean air and water,
and finally, more than 2,000 years after Aristotle, the
WHO also demands pure air and water.

Using the standard of health as expressed by the
WHO "definition" of health it appears that the WHO
is a catastrophic failure in terms of implementing
conditions according to their own "definition" of
health.

76

The WHO is failing in areas such as pollution where it would be relatively easy to heavily criticise and reprimand governments, corporations and NGOs which are the culprits for the extreme pollution of the environment.

There was a big scandal of the WHO tetanus vaccine agenda in several African states, in particular in Kenya, where allegedly an infertility function was added to the tetanus vaccine through beta HCG [59]. This could mean that population control may be on the agenda of the WHO. According to the statements of particular scientists such as Mike Yeadon, the Covid-19 vaccine may interfere with fertility through spike protein activity [59].

In Malta every year 500 people have premature death due to air pollution [60]. 28 medical and environmental organisations have stated, among other issues, that the obesity pandemic, mental health, noise and air pollution are interlinked and should receive the same attention as Covid-19 [60].

In recent times there have been claims that genetics play an important role in humans in the areas of personality, mental and social traits [61].

In the 3rd Reich the inhumane race laws were based

upon fake genetic science. In the Q & A section of the WHO website differences between genetics and genomics are explained based on the WHO's understanding that genomics has a much wider context than genetics with respect to human health [62]. This wider context of genomics and associated technologies extends the power of the WHO in a massive way. This may serve as the justification for medical tyranny on a global scale.

There was a huge programme against cancer in the 3rd Reich [63]. One may argue that the programmes fighting diseases such as cancer during the 3rd Reich were at least partially used back then to disguise the inhumane activities of the medical establishment. Under the 3rd Reich a dictatorship was established in which physicians took the lead in public health at the expense of individual liberties [63].

Public health initiatives have to be analysed within the wider framework of the symbiotic relationship between science and politics, a relationship in which the Nazis took the lead [63].

Nowadays the WHO also has programmes such as anti-cancer programmes which, in general, are not successful. One has to ask whether these WHO programmes also serve different agendas such as pretending to serve the health of nations while in reality pursuing other inhumane programmes such as population control activities. Large data bases exist such as the Cancer Incidence in 5 Continents (CI5) but despite these huge collections of data about cancer there has been no corresponding progress in finding a cure for cancer in the dominating medical model of school medicine. The WHO is failing when it comes to delivering tangible results in many areas, including fighting cancer.

In the future, mental disorders, obesity or heart failures may be used to declare pandemics. The WHO and its understanding of health as published in the so-called "definition" of health appear to have an important function in this respect.

Health and Governments

Public health administration can be used to increase control over populations and to impose industry friendly regulations and laws on populations.

In general, the increase of the state welfare systems came to a halt through the oil crisis in the 1970s [64]. A more recent study of 23 OECD countries shows that the governments' roles follow similar patterns with respect to regulations, service provisions and financing [64]. In the study mentioned above three types of health care systems were noted: private health insurance systems, social health insurance and national health insurance [64]. The researchers of the study discovered similarities shared by all three types of health care systems which exist as a consequence of developments over time [64]. One may assume that this development is indicative of a globalist approach in health care systems across many countries.

As mentioned previously, in Judaism health has priority over the religious rules, even though it is debated what justifies this special situation.

Is the health of populations also a top priority of governments?

There are numerous reports about people who were declared dead but then came to life in morgues.

In Germany in 2015 a 92 year old women was declared dead but in the evening she woke up in the refrigeration room of a morgue and was saved because her screams were heard by staff of the morgue [65]. Two days later the woman died officially a second time and on this occasion she had officially died of causes unrelated to the previous physically and psychological burdening incident [65].

Also in Germany, a 72 year old woman was taken to a morgue because the medical professionals could not detect any signs of life in her [66]. Once again, morgue staff saved the life of a patient because it was discovered that the patient was breathing [66]. At the time of the article this particular patient was in a coma in a hospital [66].

In the Philippines a toddler woke up at her funeral but died later [67].

Morgues normally have a cooling system thus limiting the chances of survival of already weakened patients, in particular if these patients are old or young.

Are these reports just showing the tip of the famous iceberg?

Can this be excused by incompetence or neglect?

Could this be foul play?

Governments and the WHO are also failing in the area of death certificates. This could easily be avoided.

The dinosaur media, governments, NGOs and large corporations act in concert when it comes to producing long term stress for individuals and populations. Themes used to produce fear include subjects such as depression, inflation, unemployment, increasing crime rates, illegal immigration, increased rates for neurodegenerative diseases, increased rates for chronic diseases, infectious diseases, shortages, terrorism and war. The presentation of a scapegoat which is persistently presented to the public as a threat may also produce long term stress. These themes can be presented in a way that considerably increases long term stress. Long term stress may cause symptoms such as deterioration in health, infertility, a suppressed immune system and probably cancer as a consequence of a decreased immune system [68]. According to Selye, the secretion of glucocorticoids over a long period of time is causing negative effects [68], [69]. Muscle tissues can be damaged and high blood pressure, which may lead to stroke and heart attacks, may also be observed as negative effects [68]. Brain damage may also be caused by long term exposure to high levels of glucocorticoids [68]. The symptoms may include memory loss and slower learning capabilities [68]. These symptoms have been observed in a study by Lupien et al (1996) of elderly people with higher levels of glucocorticoids compared to elderly people with normal levels [68], [70]. The situation of an individual may be worsened by post-traumatic stress disorder, and psychological distress of high intensity may be observed as a symptom [68].

Some symptoms may be caused by exposure to long term stress and some symptoms may be caused through the genetic treatments which are marketed as "vaccines" but are identical or at least are very similar. This means that the population is hit twice, first by the long term exposure to stress and then a second time by the symptoms caused by the genetic treatments marketed as "vaccinations". Both situations are capable of causing similar or identical symptoms, thereby worsening the health situations of individuals and populations. These situations may, in fact, be deliberately coordinated activities and the public has difficulty seeing the connections. The symptoms may at least partially be deliberately produced symptoms.

It is bad enough that in general the situation in public health appears to be worsening worldwide; at the same time public health is getting more expensive. The data for the USA in the table below show health care spending as a percent of GDP was way above the health expenditure for the OECD38.

Health Expenditure for 2019 [71]	
	% of GDP (estimates)
USA	16.8
Germany	11.7
United Kingdom	10.2
OECD38	8.8
Luxembourg	5.4

In 2008 the economic crisis led to a contraction of the economies of the member states of the OECD [71]. Health expenditure was maintained for a short period of time and then it also decreased [71]. Between 2010 and 2012 the growth of health expenditure was slightly above zero [71]. The USA had the highest value for health expenditure as a percentage of GDP, followed by Germany but there is a distinct gap between these two values [71].

The Covid-19 crises led to an increase of health expenditure [71]. According to an estimate from the OECD the percentage of GDP for Germany will increase to 12.5% [71]. One may assume that other economies will follow this trend.

Measures in public health such as extensive lockdowns restricted private spending and also crippled the outputs of economies [71]. In 2020 a large number of the OCED economies were forced into a freefall [71]. While GDP per capita exceeded a decrease on average of 4.5%, the pandemic led to an increase in health expenditure, in particular of the governments [71]. Based on preliminary figures, growth per capita for health expenditure may be around 5% for some member states of the OECD and analysing the last 15 years this will probably be the most accelerated increase in health spending for that period [71].

A higher ratio for health care expenditure does not necessarily mean that the quality of the service has improved nor does it necessarily mean that more people of a particular population are receiving cover for health care services.

Malta is a tiny state and health expenditure as a percent of GDP is close to the figure for Global Health Expenditure in 2015.

Health Expenditure (2015) [72]		
	% of GDP	USD
Malta	9.6	
Global	10	7.2 trillion

In 2015 global health expenditure in USD had already reached an astronomical size as shown in the table above and the trend of increasing health expenditure is shown in the table below with the example of Malta.

The table below shows that for Malta total health expenditure per capita had almost tripled from

2000 to 2015. Considering that Malta is a tiny island state with a small population and substantial benefits from its membership in the European Union, this trend may be similar in developed countries, or even worse in larger developed countries.

Malta [[73], [74], [75]				
	2000	2005	2010	2015
Total health expenditure per capita in 2011 PPP international USD inflation adjusted to 2011 USD	1,199	1,941	2,290	3,471

Luxembourg and Malta amongst other states of the EU may be in a special situation in the sense that they receive benefits from the EU which might have the intention to entice them to stay in the EU. In addition, their economic situations may be different from other member states of the EU.

The dramatic increase of health care expenditure in developed countries serves the interests of large corporations and NGOs. As the majority of the populations have to spend higher and higher percentages per capita on health care their financial capabilities become more restricted. This is also serving the transfer of money from the bottom to the top in society. Expenditure for health care can be used to force economic and political developments in certain directions desired by large corporations and NGOs. The individual becomes more and more restricted by being forced to pay contributions into failing health and social care systems. The health care systems in certain developed countries such as Germany are connected to the unemployment insurance and pension system, thereby enforcing a rigid control system on the populations. The health care systems now also serve as controlling systems for the technocrats. The digitalisation and the sharing of data across private companies and across borders serve the commercialisation of health care and do not have health at the centre of corporate activities. Confidential health care data are now available to private corporations. The availability of patient data is moving power to the large corporations and NGOs as the data can be used for analysis, marketing and all types of insurance sections, including health, life, motor, unemployment and mortgage insurance.

Many politicians act in their own interests and they are also the poodles of large corporations and NGOs. The financial system ensures that large corporations and NGOs have plenty of money available for legally influencing or bribing politicians and other leaders. The proposed Great Reset of the World Economic Forum would make it even easier to enslave the majority of the world's population since everything and everyone would be under control.

Corruption is currently endemic in all areas of health care systems all over the globe [76]. In this situation free markets are abolished and oligarchies or even monopolies are established.

Big pharma consists of a few large corporations and the big fund managers such as BlackRock and Vanguard hold shares of each other so that it is clear that they have similar or even identical interests. This means that a never before existing concentration of power in the hands of a few is causing problems and harm to the majority of people worldwide.

The Rockefeller medicine war on cancer has been lost and one has to wonder why there has been no substantial progress despite substantial amounts of money having been given from governments and NGOs to fund cancer research.

Health care funding is in competition with the funding of other governmental departments, most notably with the military industrial complex.

In 1971 president Nixon took the US off of the gold standard [77]. The hidden reason for the removal of the gold standard was that the US could no longer disguise the extremely high expenditure for the war in Vietnam [77]. The US had dramatically increased the amount of printing dollars [77].

In 2015 in the UK the design and manufacture of four submarines was estimated to be £31 billion [78]. This was £6 billion over the initial estimate in 2011 [78]. In this context the final expenses tend to be much higher than the original estimates and there are also maintenance costs for such programmes. This is just the estimate for one programme of the military complex in the UK.

In the US in 2010 the Affordable Care Act, also referred to as Obamacare, introduced the largest changes to health care policy since 1965 [79]. Obamacare has been heavily criticised on numerous grounds [79]. The cover of the health insurance increased mainly by the expansion of Medicaid, with about 6 million people losing their insurance cover [79]. Support for people who are working and people in the middle class is decreasing [79]. Under Obamacare there is no help for two fifths of the population [79]. Employers have decreased health benefits for their workers [79]. Out of pocket payments for health care have increased for certain groups [79]. Accessing health care is not evenly distributed throughout the population [79].

Health care is confronted with many problems and there are also problems involving horrendous crimes which profoundly disturb the official picture of the relationship between patient and health care practitioner.

In the UK a general practitioner with the name of Dr Shipman killed more than 215 patients [80]. Dr Shipman was able to to commit these crimes over a period of 34 years until his criminal carrier was finally stopped [80]. This case has to be discussed in public and all related issues should be solved, including a failing health system, the damaged doctor patient relationship, the trust between medical staff, the lack of accountability and how to prevent such a case from reoccurring [80].

Death certificates, cremation certificates, coroners' services, controlled drugs and whistleblowing are also relevant issues for such cases but despite all the areas involved the state health system has failed miserably [81]. The state health care system has failed to develop a mechanism which can detect such crimes. One has to question whether there are similar cases out there, and if so, how many, and why the health care system is also failing in this important issue.

Other serious problems which impact upon the health of people exist but they are not discussed within the framework of this book. Here are just a few examples.

Contamination of food with pathogens such as Salmonella through the industrialised production of meat and eggs has been observed quite often.

Fruits and vegetables produced in depleted soil have low quality in terms of reduced content of minerals and vitamins.

The use of herbicides and pesticides may have long-lasting negative effects on human health.

The expenditure for health care exploded over the last decades. Here Malta and the US may serve as examples.

A health care professional from New York told me that if social services are informed about problems in a care case they freeze the assets of that patient in care, thereby blocking any input from caring relatives.

In 1883 one of Darwin's cousins first used the term eugenics [82]. Eugenics started in the UK and then it travelled to the USA [82]. This cousin of Darwin thought that the state should give financial incentives for marriage to individuals who he thought to be the fittest [82]. Politicians and intellectuals supported the ideas of improving society in this way [82]. Winston Churchill, Woodrow Wilson, Alexander Graham Bell and John Maynard Keynes are just a few examples of famous individuals who believed these ideas of improving society in this way [82]. Government interventions were long thought by these eugenicists to improve the human race by promoting selective breeding [82].

In reality this formed the base for forced sterilisation, sponsored discrimination and genocide [82].

In an interview Dr Vladimir Zelenko stated that the people from Sodom and Gomorrah were not condemned because of immorality but because these people enshrined immorality into their law. They made immorality legal [83].

The points mentioned above are just a few examples of big scandals in the health care services from the UK, Germany, Malta and the US.

Considering that many people working in the state health services attended universities with high reputations it is hard to believe that incompetence, ignorance, laziness and stupidity are the reasons for the gigantic failures in the health services. Is it believable to state that there are so many specialists qualifying for the title of Dr Catastrophe? The practising Dr Catastrophe does exist but in most of the big bad events this is just an excuse. It is far more likely that the bad events were done deliberately. A Dr Catastrophe may be selected by organisations such as the World Economic Forum for top positions because these Dr Catastrophes are willing to receive and follow orders. In a functioning competitive economy a Dr Catastrophe would find it difficult to find a decent job and if a Dr Catastrophe knows that, they are more likely to be willing executors of orders however unethical those orders may be.

Of course there are also decent people in the health care services but there are also many rotten apples. Corruption is a worldwide problem and there is a website from transparency.org assessing the degree of corruption in countries worldwide [76].

Conclusion

The "definition" of health provided by the WHO is not precise and it does not fulfil scientific scrutiny. It uses terms such as disease and infirmity which require scientific definitions.

Since the WHO has provided a statement about health and not a "definition" of health it has to be asked whether this provision of a statement is a deliberate act so that certain political, social and economic goals can be achieved.

A deliberately vague "definition" can be used to install political systems such as a psychiatric tyranny. Health care organisations on a global level in the form of NGOs such as the WHO have failed to provide solutions to improve health care in many areas. Health care on state and global levels are prone to corruption and misguided projects.

The establishment of oligarchies or even monopolies in the health and social care systems has shifted the balance of power further in favour of large corporations and NGOs.

This accumulation of power strongly suggests that local solutions for problems in a health care crisis will be met with strong resistance from the large global and powerful corporations and NGOs such as the WHO which are seeking more and more power. Increasing profits for the large corporations also serve the purpose of weakening competition from smaller service providers in health care. This also aids the transfer of assets from the bottom to the top. This transfer of assets can be seen as an important part in the implementation of the so-called "New World Order".

One major disadvantage of the WHO is that their mistakes and their misguided deliberate actions are global, as indicated by their name.

References

[1]
Jaynes, E. T. PROBABILITY THEORY: THE LOGIC OF SCIENCE. (2003) Part 1, Ch 9 Repetitive Experiments: probability and frequency, p. 279, Cambridge University Press, Cambridge

[2]
Beinfield, Harriet and Korngold, Efrem (2005) Traditionelle Chinesische Medizin; Deutscher Taschenbuch Verlag GmbH & Co KG; München

[3]
Tarfe, Akshay (15th June 2021) Why Are Indians So Angry at Bill Gates?
https://thediplomat.com/2021/06/why-are-indians-so-angry-at-bill-gates/
accessed: 21st June 2021

[4]
Edwards, Nancy & Di Ruggiero, Erica (2011); Exploring which context matters in the study of health inequities and their mitigation; Scandinavian Journal of Public Health; 39(Suppl 6): 43–49

[5]
Thompson, A.K.; Faith, K.; Gibson, J.L. & Upshure, R.EG (2006) Pandemic Influenza Preparedness: An ethical framework to guide decision-making; BMC Medical Ethics; 7: 12

[6]
Gibson, J.L.; Martin, D.K.; & Singer, P.A.; (8th Sep. 2004) Setting priorities in health care organizations: criteria, processes and parameters of success; BMC Health Services Research , 4:25

[7]
Moynihan, Ray; Heath, Iona and Henry, David (13th April 2002) Selling sickness: the pharmaceutical industry and disease mongering, BMJ Volume 324

[8]
United Nations Development Programme, Human Development Indices and Indicators, 2018 Statistical Update, New York, NY

[9]
Sloman, John and Garratt, Dean (2010) Essentials of Economics 5th Edn, Chapter 12 Macroeconomic policy, Pearson Education Ltd. Harlow, England

[10]
Samuelson, Paul A. and Nordhaus, William D. (2006) Economics, Chapter 20 Overview of Macroeconomics, Tata McGraw-Hill Publishing Company Ltd., New Delhi

[11]
World Health Organization, Constitution, https://www.who.int/about/governance/constitution downloaded: 22nd January 2022

[12]
Carl Jung, in: Gale Encyclopedia of Psychology (2001) 2nd Edition, Bonnie Strickland Executive editor, Gale Group, Farmington Hills, MI

[13]

Lewis, David M. (2011) WHO definition of health remains fit for purpose *general practitioner BMJ* ; 343:d5357 doi: 10.1136/bmj.d5357

[14]

Dr Glidden, Cabal's biggest secret & scam, everyone needs to know w/ Dr Glidden, interviewed by Sarah Westall video in 2020 SarahWestall.com, accessed: 10th July 2022

[15]

Davis, Ronald L.; (2020) Mechanism of Action and Target Identification: A Matter of Timing in Drug Discovery, iScience, Volume 23, Issue 9, 01487, ISSN 25890042, https://doi.org/10.1016/j.isci.2020.101487. https://www.sciencedirect.com/science/article/pii/S2589004220306799

[16]

Gaugler, J.E., Ascher-Svanum, H., Roth, D.L. *et al.* (2013) Characteristics of patients misdiagnosed with Alzheimer's disease and their medication use: an analysis of the NACC-UDS database. *BMC Geriatr* 13, 137 . https://doi.org/10.1186/1471-2318-13-137

[17]

Bendix, Aria and Chow, Denise (26th July 2022) 12:12 AM CEST; Allegations of fabricated research undermine key Alzheimer's theory, https://www.nbcnews.com/science/science-news/alzheimers-theory-undermined-accusations-fabricated-research-rcna39843

[18]
Moncrieff, J., Cooper, R.E., Stockmann, T. *et al.* (20th July 2022) The serotonin theory of depression: a systematic umbrella review of the evidence. *Mol Psychiatry*

[19]
European Union Agency for Fundamental Rights, https://fra.europa.eu/en/eu-charter/article/35-health-care
downloaded: 22nd April 2022

[20]
White, P.D. & Clare, A.W.; Psychological Medicine; in: Kumar, P. & Clark, M.; (2009) Clinical Medicine 7th Edn.; Saunders Elsevier; pp. 1185-1224

[21]
About DSM-5-TR
https://psychiatry.org/psychiatrists/practice/dsm/about-dsm,
accessed: 11th September 2022

[22]
American Psychiatric Association, Diagnostic and Statistical Manual of Mental Disorders, 5th Edition, Arlington, VA, 2013, page 66

[23]
American Psychiatric Association, Diagnostic and Statistical Manual of Mental Disorders, 5th Edition, Arlington, VA, 2013, page 66-74

[24]
vocabulary.com, online dictionary, https://www.vocabulary.com/dictionary/infirmity

downloaded: 22nd January 2022

[25]
medical dictionary, https://medicalictionary.thefree
dictionary.com/infirmities
downloaded : 22nd January 2022

[26]
Leviticus 18.5, Vayikra - Leviticus
Torah – The Pentateuch The Complete Jewish
Bible, With RashioCommentary https://www.ch
abad.org/library/bible_cdo/aid/9919/jewish/
accessed: 12th September 2022

[27]
Ezekiel 20:11
The   Complete   Jewish   Bible,   With   Rashi
Commentary, https://www.chabad.org/library/bible_
cdo/aid/16118/jewish/Chapter-20.htm
accessed: 12th September 2022

[28]
Mark 2.17, Scripture4all Foundation (© 2010)
www.scripture4all.org
accessed: 12thSeptember2022

[29]
Clarke, Thomas., Ed. (2004) Theories of Corporate
Governance, The philosophical foundations of
corporate governance, Routledge, New York, NY

[30]
McEwan, Michael, The shameful legacy of the
Lennox Castle Hospital

https://www.bbc.com/news/uk-scotland-glasgow-west-59755040
accessed: 2nd April 2022

[31]
Borland, B. (16th September 2017) Names of buried disabled children unearthed in mass graves revealed, https://www.express.co.uk/news/uk/855064/scotland-Lennox-Castle-Hospital-patients-bodies-buried-graves

[32]
Salize, Hans J.; Dreßing, Harald and Peitz, Monika (2002) Compulsory Admission and Involuntary Treatment of Mentally Ill Patients-Legislation and Practice in EU-Member States, Final Report, https://ec.europa.eu/health/ph_projects/2000/promotion/fp_promotion_2000_frep_08_en.pdf
accessed: 9th June 2022

[33]
Kokkonen P. (1993). Coercion and Legal Protection in Psychiatric Care in Finland. *Medicine and Law*, *12*(1-2), 113–124.

[34]
Malcolm L. (1989): Bed availability as a significant influence on rates of committal to New Zealand's psychiatric hospitals. New Zealand Medical Journal 102: 8-9

[35]
Gendreau C. (1997): The Rights of Psychiatric Patients in the Light of the Principles Announced by the United Nations. International Journal of Law and Psychiatry 20: 259-78

[36]
Harding TW (2000): Human rights law in the field of mental health: a critical review. Acta Psychiatrica Scandinavica 101: 24-30

[37]
Wachenfeld MG (1991): The Human Rights of the Mentally Ill in Europe. Nordic Journal of International Law 60: 110-92

[38]
Mahler H, Co BT (1984): Who are the "Committed"? Update. Journal of Nervous and Mental Disease 172:189-96

[39]
Riecher A, Rössler W, Löffler W, Fätkenheuer B (1991): Factors influencing compulsory admission of psychiatric patients. Psychological Medicine 21: 197-208

[40]
Spengler A (1986): Factors influencing assignment of patients to compulsory admission. Social Psychiatry 21: 113-22

[41]
Rath, Christian (2020) Endete der Kampf für Grundrechte in der Psychiatrie?: Anwältin Beate Bahner ist wieder frei . In: Legal Tribune Online, 17.04.2020 https://www.lto.de/recht/hintergruende/h/rechtsanwaeltin-bahner-heidelberg-corona-skepsis-grdunrechte-psychiatrie-verschwoerung/ accessed: 9th June 2022

[42]
openpetition (2020)
https://www.openpetition.de/petition/online/umfassende-aufklaerung-der-im-beate-bahner-audio-erhobenen-vorwuerfe-von-u-a-polizeigewalt
accessed: 9th June 2022

[43]
Goldhagen, Daniel Jonah (1996) Hitler's Willing Executioners, Ordinary Germans and the Holocaust, Little, Brown and Company; London, UK p 270

[44]
Goldhagen, Daniel Jonah (1996) Hitler's Willing Executioners, Ordinary Germans and the Holocaust, Little, Brown and Company; London, UK
text pages 232- 233, index pages 615 – 617

[45]
Goldhagen, Daniel Jonah (1996) Hitler's Willing Executioners, Ordinary Germans and the Holocaust, Little, Brown and Company; London, UK

[46]
Learmount, Simon (2002) Theorizing Corporate Governance: New Organizational Alternatives, Working Papers Centre for Business Research, University of Cambridge

[47]
Marcuse, Herbert, (1964) One Dimensional Man; Studies in the Ideology of Advanced Industrial Society. Routledge New York, NY,. Reprinted 2007, pp 209-10, 212, 213, 223

[48]

Stromberg, Joseph (1st March 2013) What Does the Unbelievably Bad Air Quality in Beijing Do to the Human Body?
http://blogs.smithsonianmag.com/science/
accessed: 29th May 2013

[49]

Guo, Yuming; Zeng, Hongmei; Zheng, Rongshou; Li, Shanshan; Barnett, Adrian G.; Zhang, Siwei; Zou, Xiaonong; Huxley, Rachel and Chen, Wanqing The association between lung cancer incidence and ambient air pollution in China: A spatiotemporal analysis, Environmental Research Volume 144, Part A, January 2016, Pages 60-65, https://www.sciencedirect.com/science/article/abs/pii/S0013935115301341?via%3Dihub
https://doi.org/10.1016/j.envres.2015.11.004Get rights and content

[50]

International Agency for Research on Cancer. 470-Malta-fact-sheet, WHO, The Global Cancer Observatory - All Rights Reserved - March, 2021
https://gco.iarc.fr/today/data/factsheets/populations/470-malta-fact-sheets.pdf
downloaded 11th August 2022

[51]

UN, United Nations, International decade for Action 'Water for Life' 2005-2015 ,
https://www.un.org/waterforlifedecade/human_right_to_water.shtml
accessed: 5th August 2022

[52]
WHO, Global Reference List of 100 Core Health
Indicators, 2018 Edition

[53]
Farrugia, Claire (16th January 2020)   Malta's tap
water linked to fifth of bladder cancer cases,
Situation in Malta among the worst in Europe
https://timesofmalta.com/articles/view/maltas-tap-
water-linked-to-fifth-of-bladder-cancer-
cases.763824

[54]
Ganado, Philip Leone (14th March 2019) Air quality
deaths in Malta more than twice than previously
thought - 800,000 people a year across the EU die
early due to air pollution
https://timesofmalta.com/articles/view/air-quality-
deaths-in-malta-more-than-twice-than-previously-
thought.704455,
accessed: 4th June 2021

[55]
OECD/European Observatory on Health Systems
and Policies (2021), Malta: Country Health Profile
2021, State of Health in the EU, OECD Publishing,
Paris/European Observatory on Health Systems and
Policies, Brussels.
downloaded 28th August 2022

[56]
World Health Organization. *World Health Statistics
2018: Monitoring Health for the SDGs, Sustainable
Development Goals.* Geneva : s.n., 2018. ISBN 978-
92-4-156558-5

[57]
Globocan. [Online] March 2019.
cited: 2nd December 2019

[58]
Aristotle, Politics, translated by Rackham, H.
(MCMLIX) William Heinemann Ltd, London, UK
reprinted 1959, page 587

[59]
Wakefield, Andy (2022), Video, Infertility: A
diabolical agenda, A Children's Health Defence
Film, Executive Producer Robert F. Kennedy, Jr.

[60]
MAPHM Administrator, Air Pollution costing the
life of more than one person a day in Malta, Times
of Malta, https://maphm.org/2020/05/16/air-
pollution-costing-the-life-of-more-than-one-person-
a-day-in-malta/ Air Pollution costing the life of more
than one person a day in Malta
accessed 16th May 2020

[61]
Allen, Garland E., (2002) The Ideology of
Elimination: American and German Eugenics, 1900-
1945; in Medicine and medical ethics in Nazi
Germany

[62]
WHO, 2020: WHO, Genomics
https://www.who.int/news-room/questions-and-
answers/item/genomics
accessed: 3rd July 2022

[63]
Proctor, Robert N. (2002) The Nazi Campaign Against Tobacco: Science in a Totalitarian State; in Medicine and Medical Ethics in Nazi German

[64]
Schmid, Achim; Cacace, Mirella; Götze, Ralf; Rothgang, Heinz (2010) Explaining Health Care System Change: Problem Pressure and the Emergence of "Hybrid" Health Care Systems Journal of Health Politics, Policy and Law, Vol. 35, No. 4, August 2010 DOI 10.1215/03616878-2010-013 © 2010 by Duke University Press

[65]
independent (29th July 2015) NewsWorldEurope Woman declared dead by doctors in Germany wakes up in funeral home - Doctor charged with negligent bodily harm after allegedly pronouncing seriously-ill woman dead
https://www.independent.co.uk/news/world/europe/woman-declared-dead-by-doctors-in-germany-wakes-up-in-funeral-home-10423221.html, accessed: 9th June 2022

[66]
Collis, Helen (3rd September 2013) Woman declared dead at German crash scene is discovered hours later alive in morgue
https://www.dailymail.co.uk/news/article-2410040/Woman-declared-dead-German-crash-scene-discovered-hours-later-ALIVE-morgue.html accessed: 9th June 2022

[67]
Huffington Post UK, (15th July 2014) 'Dead' Filipino Toddler Who 'Awoke' At Her Own Funeral Has Been Pronounced Dead Again https://www.huffingtonpost.co.uk/2014/07/15/dead-child-comes-back-to-life-funeral-pronounced-dead-again_n_5587066.html accessed: 9th June 2022

[68]
Carlson, Neil R. Physiology of Behavior (2001) Chapter 18 Anxiety Disorders, Autistic Disorder, and Stress Disorder pp. 557 – 581, Allyn and Bacon a Pearson Education Company

[69]
Selye (1976) as referred to in Carlson, Neil R. Physiology of Behavior (2001) Chapter 18 Anxiety Disorders, Autistic Disorder, and Stress Disorder pp. 557 – 581, Allyn and Bacon a Pearson Education Company

[70]
Lupien et al (1996), as referred to in Carlson, Physiology of Behaviour, 2001

[71]
OECD Health Statistics 2021, WHO Global Health Expenditure Database https://www.oecd-ilibrary.org/sites/e26f669c-en/index.html?itemId=/content/component/e26f669c-en#indicator-d1e10346 accessed: 12th August 2022

[72]
World Health Organization, www.who.int/gho/heal

th_financing/health_expenditure/en/

[73]
World Bank Data Help Desk. What is the difference between current and constant data?

[74]
World Bank Data Help Desk. What is an "international dollar"?

[75]
World Health Organization. Global Health Expenditure Database. Data Explorer. Set up a table by selecting options in the left sidebar. Then click "view data and build report" to get a table with year columns, and country rows.

[76]
Transparency.org,
https://www.transparency.org/en/ourpriorities/health-and-corruption
accessed 5th April 2022

[77]
Redman, Jamie (15th August 2021) The 50th Anniversary of 'Nixon Shock:' How Suspending the Dollar's Convertibility With Gold Fueled Today's Fiat World https://news.bitcoin.com/the-50th-anniversary-of-nixon-shock-how-suspending-the-dollars-convertibility-with-gold-fueled-todays-fiat-world/
accessed 9th June 2022

[78]
Mills, Clair and Dempsey, Noel; (update 2nd March 2021) The Cost of the UK's Strategic Nuclear

Deterrent, Briefing Paper Number 8166, www.parliament.uk/commons-library intranet.parliament.uk/commons-library

[79]
Manchikanti, Laxmaiah; Helm II, Standiford; Benyamin, Ramsin M. and Hirsch, Joshua A. (2017) A Critical Analysis of Obamacare: Affordable Care or Insurance for Many and Coverage for Few? Pain Physician 2017; 20:111-138

[80]
Baker, R. (2004) Postgraduate Med J., 80, 303-306, Herold Shipman: The aftermath, Implications of Harold Shipman for general practice

[81]
Jackson, Trevor and Smith, Richard (24th January 2004) BMJ Volume 328, Obituaries, Harold Shipman, A general practitioner and murderer

[82]
Farber, Steven A. (2008) U.S. Scientists' Role in the Eugenics Movement (1907–1939): A Contemporary Biologist's Perspective ZEBRAFISH Volume 5, Number 4, 2008

[83]
Zelenko, Dr Vladimir, interview with Sarah Westall, First published at 00:13 UTC on March 21st, 2022 Jew's True Calling, Khazarian Mafia's Scapegoat, Evil Manifested Today w/ Dr. Zelenko (1of2) Free Your Mind https://www.bitchute.com/video/C51MlFHqZIBU/ accessed 5th April 2022

www.ingramcontent.com/pod-product-compliance
Lightning Source LLC
Chambersburg PA
CBHW070158290526
45789CB00002B/825